1

2

3

Holy Spirit of Love

By

John C Burt.

4

Photographs Courtesy of :

martin - pechy.

neal - e - johnson.

steve - halama.

thomas - kinto.

christopher-campbell.

zach - ahmajani.

Free downloads on :

unsplash.com

6

7

8

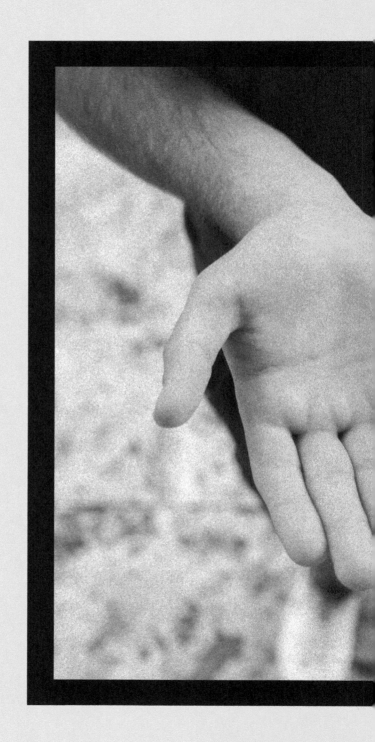

9

10

11

12

13

14

15

16

17

1.

FOREWORD :

It may seem to be obvious to you all that the ' Holy

18

Spirit of Love ' is the title of this book and one of the main qualities of the Holy Spirit? Yet, it seems important to restate this again, at times we can so

19

easily forget this very important truth. In our days and in our generations the focus of anything to do with the Holy Spirit is on, largely, the power

20

of the Holy Spirit? I have no problem with that, per say, but I do also believe that we need to understand the love aspect of the Holy Spirit and His being ...

21

poured out after the Lord Jesus Christ , had ascended back to the Father in Heaven. It's all too easy to overlook the very reality of the Holy

Spirit been given and empowered by the LOVE of the trinity; the Father , the Son of God and the Holy Spirit Himself.

As 1 Corinthians does say, it is Love

is the one thing that is eternal and remains out of the three Faith, Hope and LOVE.

Also, my focus on this aspect is because there is at times not enough

24

space and even air
- time given to
LOVE and the
Holy Spirit within
the Body of
Christ
Worldwide?

28

29

31

36

37

2.

Now we come to the citations from the Word of God. There will be four different versions of the texts given. They will be the NIV, the ESV, the GNT and the Voice versions of the Word.

38

(NIV)
John 14 : 15 - 19.

" (15) " If you love me, keep my commands.

(16) And I will ask the Father, and he will give you another advocate to

help you and be
with you forever -
(17) the
Spirit of truth. The
world cannot
accept him,
because it neither
sees him nor
knows him. But you

40

know him, for he lives with you and will be in you.

(18) I will not leave you as orphans; I will come to you.

(19) Before long, the world will not see me anymore,

but you will see me.
Because I live, you
also will live. " "

John 15 : 26.
" (26) " When
the Advocate
comes, whom I will
send to you from

42

the Father - the Spirit
of truth who goes out
from the Father - he
will testify about
me.""

Romans 5 : 5
"(5) And hope
does not put us to
shame, because

43

God's love has been poured out into our hearts through the Holy Spirit, who has been given to us."

Romans 8 : 15 - 16.

" (15) The Spirit

44

you received does not make you slaves, so that you live in fear again; rather, the Spirit you received brought about your adoption to sonship. And by him we cry, " Abba, Father."

(16) The Spirit himself testifies with our spirit that we are God's children."

Romans 8 : 26 - 27.

"(26) In the same way, the Spirit

46

helps us in our weakness. We do not know what we ought to pray for, but the Spirit himself intercedes for through wordless groans.

(27) And he who searches our

hearts knows the mind of the Spirit, because the Spirit intercedes for God's people in accordance with the will of God."

1 Corinthians 2 : 6 - 16.

48

" (6) We do, however, speak a message of wisdom among the mature, but not the wisdom of this age or of the rulers of this age, who are coming to nothing.

49

(7) No, we declare God's wisdom, a mystery that has been hidden and that God destined for our glory before time began.

(8) None of the

rulers of this age understood it, for if they had , they would not have crucified the Lord of glory.

(9) However, as it is written :

" What no eye has

seen, what no ear has heard, and what no human mind has conceived" - the things God has prepared for those who love him -

(10) these are the things God

has revealed to us by his Spirit.

The Spirit searches all things, even the deep things of God.

(11) For who knows a person's thoughts except their own spirit within them?

In the same way no one knows the thoughts of God except the Spirit of God.

(12) What we have received is not the spirit of the world, but the

Spirit who is from God. so that we may understand what God has freely given us.

(13) This is what we speak, not in words taught us by human wisdom but in words taught by the Spirit, explaining

spiritual realities with Spirit - taught words.

(14) The person without the Spirit does not accept the things that come from the Spirit of God but considers them foolishness, and

56

cannot understand them because they are discerned only through the Spirit.

(15) The person with the Spirit makes judgments about all such things, but such a person is not

subject to merely human judgments, (16) for," Who has known the mind of the Lord so as to instruct him?" But we have the mind of Christ."

1 Corinthians 3 : 16 - 17.

" (16) Don't you know that you yourselves are God's temple and that God's Spirit dwells in your midst?

(17) If anyone destroys God's temple,

God will destroy that person; for God's temple is scared, and you together are that temple."

1 Corinthians 6 : 19 - 20.

" (19) Do you not know that your

60

bodies are temples of the Holt Spirit, who is in you, whom you have received from God? You are not your own;

(20) you were bought at a price. Therefore honor God with your bodies."

1 Corinthians 12 : 3.

"(3) Therefore I want you to know that no one who is speaking by the Spirit of God says, " Jesus be cursed," and no one can say, " Jesus is Lord,"

62

except by the Holy Spirit."

1 Corinthians 13 : 1 - 3.

"(1) If I speak in the tongues of men or of angels, but do not have love, I am only a resounding gong or a clanging cymbal.

(2) If I have the gift of prophecy and can fathom all mysteries and all knowledge, and if I have a faith that can move mountains, but do not have love, I am nothing.

(3) If I give all I possess to the poor and give over my body to hardship that I may boast, but do not have love, I gain nothing. "

2 Corinthians 5 : 5

" (5) Now the one who has fashioned us for this very purpose is God, who has given us the Spirit as a deposit, guaranteeing what is to come."

66

Galatians 5 : 16 - 18.

"(16) So I say, walk by the Spirit, and you will not gratify the desires of the flesh.

(17) For the flesh desires what is contrary to the Spirit, and the Spirit what

is contrary to the flesh. They are in conflict with each other, so that you are not to do whatever you want.

(18) But if you are led by the Spirit, you are not under the law."

Galatians 5 : 22 - 23.

" (22) But the fruit of the Spirit is love,joy, peace, forbearance, kindness, goodness, faithfulness,

(23) gentleness and self - control. Against such things there is no law."

2 Timothy 1 : 14.

" (14) Guard the good deposit that was entrusted to you - guard it with the help of the Holy Spirit who lives in us."

70

1 John 4 : 12 - 13.

" (12) No one has ever seen God; but if we love one another, God lives in us and his love is made complete in us.

(13) This is how we know that we live in he in us : He has given us of his Spirit."

71

72

73

74

76

77

78

3.

(ESV)

John 14 : 15 - 19.

"(15) " If you love me, you will keep my commandments. (16) And I will ask the Father, and he will give yo another Helper, to be with you forever, (17) even the Spirit of truth, whom the world cannot receive, because it neither sees him nor knows him. You know him, for he dwells with you and will be in you.

(18) " I will not leave you as orphans; I will come to you.

(19) Yet a little while and the world will see me no

more, but you will see me. Because I live, you also will live." "

John 15 : 26.
" (26)" But when the Helper comes, whom I will send to you from the Father, the Spirit of truth,

who proceeds from the Father, he will bear witness about me."

Romans 5 : 5.

" (5) and hope does not put us to shame, because God's love has been

poured into our
hearts through the
Holy Spirit who has
been given to us."

Romans 8 : 15 -
16.

"(15) For you
did not receive the
spirit of slavery to

fall back into fear,
but you have
received the Spirit of
adoption as sons, by
whom we cry,
" Abba! Father! "
(16) The
Spirit himself bears
witness with our
spirit that we are

children of God,"

Romans 8 : 26 - 27.
"(26) Likewise the Spirit helps us in our weakness. For we do not know what to pray for as we ought, but the Spirit himself intercedes

for us with groanings too deep for words. (27) And he who searches hearts knows what is the mind of the Spirit, because the Spirit intercedes for the saints according to the will of God. "

88

1 Corinthians 2 : 6 - 16.

"(6) Yet among the mature we do impart wisdom, although it is not a wisdom of this age or of the rulers of this age, who are doomed to pass away.

89

(7) But we impart a secret and hidden wisdom of God, which God decreed before the ages for our glory.

(8) None of the rulers of this age understood this, for

if they had, they would not have crucified the Lord of glory.

(9) But, as it is written,

" What no eye has seen, nor ear heard, nor the heart

of man imagined, what God has prepared for those who love him" -
            (10) these things God has revealed to us through the Spirit. For the Spirit searches everything, even the

92

depths of God.

(11) For who knows a person's thoughts except the spirit of that person, which is in him? So also no one comprehends the thoughts of God except the Spirit of

God.

    (12) Now we have not received not the spirit of the world, but the Spirit who is from God, that we might understand the things freely given us by God.

94

(13) And we impart this in words not taught by human wisdom but taught by the Spirit, interpreting spiritual truths to those who are spiritual. (14) The natural person does

not accept the things of the Spirit of God, for they are folly to him, and he is not able to understand them because they are spiritually discerned.

(15) The spiritual person judges all

things, but is himself
to be judged by no
one.

(16) " For who
has understood the
mind of the Lord so
as to instruct him?"
But we have the
mind of Christ."

97

1 Corinthians 3 : 16 - 17.

"(16) Do you not know that you are God's temple and that God's Spirit dwells in you?

(17) If anyone destroys

98

God's temple, God will destroy him. For God's temple is holy, and you are that temple."

1 Corinthians 6 : 19 - 20.

" (19) Or do

you not know that
your body is a
temple of the Holy
Spirit within you,
whom you have from
God? you are not
your own,

(20) for you
were bought with a
price. So glorify God

100

in your body."

 1 Corinthians 12 : 3.
       " (3) Therefore
 I want you to
understand that no
one speaking in the
Spirit of God ever
says " Jesus is
accursed!" and no

101

one can say " Jesus is Lord " except in the Holy Spirit."

 1 Corinthians 13 : 1 - 3.

"(1) If I speak in the tongues of men and of angels, but have not love, I am a noisy gong or a clanging cymbal.

(2) And if I have prophetic powers, and understand all mysteries and all knowledge, and if I have all faith, so as to remove mountains, but have

not love, I am nothing.

(3) If I give away all I have, and if I deliver up my body to be burned , but have not love, I gain nothing. "

2 Corinthians 5 : 5.

104

" (5) He who has prepared us for this very thing is God, who has given us the Spirit as a guarantee."

Galatians 5 : 16 - 18

" (16) But I say, walk by the Spirit, and you will not gratify the desires of the flesh. (17) For the desires of the flesh are against the Spirit, and the desires of the Spirit are against the flesh, for these are opposed to each other, to keep you from doing the things you want to do.

(18) But if you are led by the Spirit, you are not

under the law. "

Galatians 5 : 22 - 23.
"(22) But the fruit of the Spirit is love, joy, peace, patience, kindness, goodness, faithfulness,

(23) gentleness, self - control; against such things there is no law."

2 Timothy 1 : 14.
" (14) By the Holy Spirit who dwells within us, guard the good

deposit entrusted to you."

1 John 4 : 12 - 13.
" (12) No one has ever seen God; if we love one another, God abides in us and his love is perfected in us.

110

(13) By this we know that we abide in him and he in us, because he has given us of his Spirit."

113

115

117

118

119

4.

(GNT)

John 14 : 15 - 19.

" (15) " If you love me, you will obey my commandments.

120

(16) I will ask the Father, and he will give you another Helper, who will stay with you forever.

(17) He is the Spirit, who reveals the truth about God. The world cannot receive him, because

it cannot see him or know him. But you know him, because he remains with you and is in you.

(18) " When I go, you will not be left all alone; I will come back to you.

(19) In a little while the world will see me no more, but you will see me; and because I live, you also will live." "

John 15 : 26.
" (26) " The

Helper will come - the Spirit, who reveals the truth about God and who comes from the Father. I will send him to you from the Father, and he will speak about me." "

124

Romans 5 : 5.

" (5) This hope does not disappoint us, for God has poured out his love into our hearts by means of the Holy Spirit, who is God's gift to us."

Romans 8 : 15 -
16.

" (15) For the
Spirit that God has
given you does not
make you slaves
and cause you to be
afraid; instead, the
Spirit makes you

God's children, and by the Spirit's power we cry out to God, " Father! my Father! "

(16) God's Spirit joins himself to our spirits to declare that we are God's children."

Romans 8 : 26 - 27.

" (26) In the same way the Spirit also comes to help us, weak as we are. For we do not know how we ought to pray; the Spirit himself pleads with God for us in groans that words cannot express.

(27) And God, who sees into our hearts, knows what the thought of the Spirit is; because the Spirit pleads with God on behalf of his people and in ....

accordance with his will."

1 Corinthians 2 : 6 - 16.

" (6) Yet I do proclaim a message of wisdom to those who are spiritually mature. But it is not the wisdom that belongs to this world or to the powers that rule this world - powers that are losing their power.

(7) The wisdom I proclaim is God's secret wisdom, which is hidden from human

beings , but which he had already chosen for our glory even before the world was made.

(8) None of the rulers of this world knew this wisdom. If they had known it, they would

not have crucified the Lord of glory.

(9) However, as the scripture says, " What no one ever saw or heard, what no one ever thought could happen, is the very thing God prepared for those

who love him."

(10) But it was to us that God made known his secret by means of his Spirit. The Spirit searches everything, even the hidden depths of God's purposes.

(11) It is only our own spirit within us that knows all about us; in the same way, only God's Spirit knows all about God.

(12) We have not received this world's spirit;

instead , we have received the Spirit sent by god, so that we may know all that God has given us.

(13) So then, we do not speak in words taught by human wisdom, but

in words taught by the Spirit, as we explain spiritual truths to those who have the Spirit.

(14) Whoever does not have the Spirit cannot receive the gifts that come

from God's Spirit.
Such a person really
does not understand
them, and they seem
to be nonsense,
because their value
can be judged only
on a spiritual basis.
(15) Whoever

has the Spirit, however, is able to judge the value of everything, but no one is able to judge him.

(16) As the scripture says,

" Who knows the mind of the Lord? Who is able to give

him advice ?"

　　We, however, have the mind of Christ." "

1 Corinthians 3 : 16 - 17.

　　" (16) Surely you know that you are God's temple

and that God's Spirit lives in you!

(17) God will destroy anyone who destroys God's temple. For God's temple is holy, and you yourselves are his temple."

1 Corinthians 6 : 19 - 20.

" (19) Don't you know that your body is the temple of the Holy Spirit, who lives in you and who was given to you by God? You do not belong to yourselves but to God;

        (20) he bought you for a price. So use your bodies for God's glory."

1 Corinthians 12 : 3.

" (3) I want you to know that no one who is led by God's Spirit can say " A curse on Jesus!" and no one can confess " Jesus is Lord," without being guided by the Holy Spirit."

1 Corinthians 13 : 1 - 3.

" (1) I may be able to speak the languages of human beings and even of angels, but if I have no love, my speech is no more than a noisy gong or a clanging bell.

(2) I may have the gift of inspired preaching; I may have all knowledge and

146

understand all secrets; I may have all the faith needed to move mountains - but if I have no love, I am nothing.

(3) I may give away everything I have, and even give up my body to

be burned - but if I have no love, this does me no good."

2 Corinthians 5 : 5.
" (5) God is the one who has prepared us for this change, and he gave us his Spirit as

the guarantee of all
that he has in store
for us."

Galatians 5 : 16 - 18.
" (16) What I
say is this: let the
Spirit direct your
lives, and you will not
satisfy the desires of

the human nature.

(17) For what our human nature wants is opposed to what the Spirit wants, and what the Spirit wants is opposed to what our human nature wants. These two are enemies, and

150

this means that yo cannot do what you want to do.

(18) If the Spirit leads you, then you are not subject to the Law."

Galatians 5 : 22 - 23.

151

" (22) But the Spirit produces love, joy, peace, patience, kindness, goodness, faithfulness,

(23) humility, and self - control. There is no law against such things as these."

2 Timothy 1 : 14.

" (14)Through the power of the Holy Spirit, who lives in us, keep the good things that have been entrusted to you."

1 John 4 : 12 - 13

153

" (12) No one has ever seen God, but if we love one another, God lives in union with us, and his love is made perfect in us.

(13) We are sure that we live in union with God and

154

that he lives in union with us, because he has given us his Spirit."

156

157

159

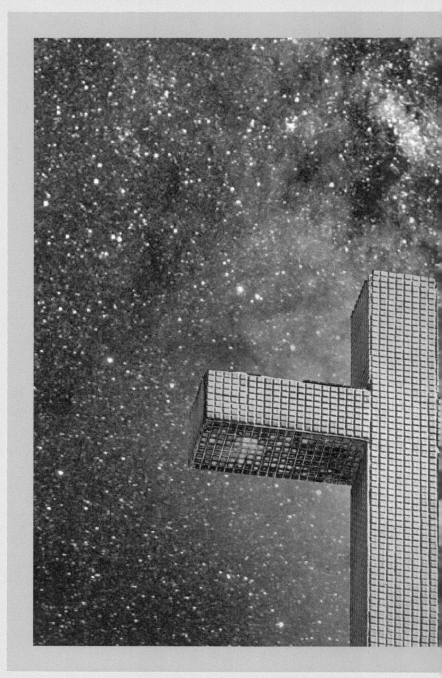

160

161

162

163

5.

(The Voice)
John 14 : 15 - 19.
(Jesus to Philip)
" (15) If you
love Me, obey the

164

commandments I have given you.

(16) I will ask the Father to send you another Helper, the Spirit of truth, who will remain constantly with you.

(17) The world does not

recognize the Spirit of truth, because it does not know the Spirit and is unable to receive Him. But you do know the Spirit because he lives with you, and He will dwell in you.

166

(18) I will never abandon you like orphans; I will return to be with you.

(19) In a little while, the world will not see Me; but I will not vanish completely from your sight.

167

Because I live, you will also live."

John 15 : 26.
" (26) I will send a great Helper to you from the Father, one known as the Spirit of truth.

168

He comes from the Father and will point to the truth as it concerns Me."

Romans 5 : 5.
" (5) And hope will never fail to satisfy our deepest need because the

Holy Spirit that was given to us has flooded our hearts with God's love."

Romans 8 : 15 - 16.
" (15) You see, you have not received a spirit that returns you to slavery

, so you have nothing to fear. The Spirit you have received adopts you and welcomes you into God's own family. That's why we call out to Him," Abba! Father! " as we would address a loving daddy. "

Romans 8 : 26 - 27.

" (26) A similar thing happens when we pray. We are weak and do not know how to pray, so the Spirit steps in and articulates prayers for us with

172

groaning too profound for words.

(27) Don't you know that He who pursues and explores the human heart intimately knows the Spirit's mind because He pleads to God for

His saints to align their lives with the will of God?"

1 Corinthians 2 : 6 - 16.

"(6) However, in the presence of mature believers, we do impart true

174

wisdom - not the phony wisdom typical of this rebellious age or of the hostile powers who rule this age. Despite what you may think, these ruling spirits are losing their grip on this world.

175

(7) But we do impart God's mysterious and hidden wisdom. Before the ages began, God graciously decided to use His wisdom for our glory. (8) This wisdom

has not been grasped by the ruling powers of this age; if they had understood, they would not have crucified the Lord of Glory.

(9) But as the Scriptures say,

No eye has ever seen and no ear has ever heard
   and it has never occurred to the human heart
   All the things God prepared for those who love Him.

178

(10) God has shown us these profound and startling realities through His Spirit. The Spirit searches all things, even the deep mysteries of God.

(11) Who can see into a man's heart and know his thoughts? Only the spirit that dwells within the man. In the same way, the thoughts of God are known only by His Spirit.

180

(12) You must know that we have not received the spirit of this rebellious and broken world but the Spirit that comes from God, so that we may experience and comprehend the gifts that come from God.

(13) We do not speak of these gifts of God in words shaped by human wisdom; we speak in words crafted by the Spirit because our collective judgment on spiritual matters is accessible to those

182

who have the Spirit.

(14) But a person who denies spiritual realities will not accept the things that come through the Spirit of God; they all sound like foolishness to him. He is incapable of grasping

them because they are disseminated, discerned, and valued by the Spirit.

(15) A person who walks by the Spirit examines everything, sizing it up and seeking out truth. But no one is

able to examine or size up that kind of spiritual person,

(16) for the Scripture asks, " Does anyone know the mind of the Lord well enough to become His advisor?" But we do

possess the mind of the Anointed One. "

1 Corinthians 3 : 16 - 17.

" (16) Don't you understand that together you form a temple to the living God and that His

186

Spirit lives among you?

(17) If someone comes along to corrupt, vandalize, and destroy the temple of God, you can be sure that God will see to it that he meets destruction

because the temple of God is sacred. You, together, are His temple."

1 Corinthians 6 : 19 - 20.

" (19) Don't you know that your

188

body is the temple of the Holy Spirit who comes from God and dwells inside of you? You do not own yourself.

(20) You have been purchased at a great price, so use

your body to bring glory to God! "

1 Corinthians 12 : 3.
" (3) With that in mind, I want you to understand that no one saying " Jesus is cursed" is operating under God's Spirit,

and no one confessing " Jesus is Lord " can do so without the Holy Spirit's inspiration."

1 Corinthians 13 : 1 - 3.

" (1) What if I speak in the most

elegant languages of people or in the exotic languages of the heavenly messengers, but I live without love? Well then, anything I say is like the clanging of brass or a crashing cymbal.

192

(2) What if I have the gift of prophecy, am blessed with knowledge and insight to all the mysteries, or what if my faith is strong enough to scoop a

mountain from its bedrock, yet I live without love? If so, I am nothing.

(3) I could give all that I have to feed the poor. I could surrender my body to be burned as a martyr, but if I do not

live in love, I gain nothing by my selfless acts."

2 Corinthians 5 : 5.
"(5) The One who has worked and tailored us for this is God Himself, who has gifted His Spirit

195

to us as a pledge toward our permanent home. "

Galatians 5 : 16 - 18. " (16) Here's my instruction : walk in the Spirit, and let the Spirit bring order to your life. If you do, you will never give in to your selfish and sinful cravings.

(17) For everything the flesh desires goes against the Spirit, and everything the Spirit desires goes against the flesh. There is a

constant battle raging between them that prevents you from doing the good you want to do.

(18) But when you are led by the Spirit, you are no longer subject to the law."

198

Galatians 5 : 22 - 23.
" (22) The Holy Spirit produces a different kind of fruit: unconditional love, joy, peace, patience, kindheartedness, goodness, faithfulness,

(23) gentleness, and self - control. You won't find any law opposed to fruit like this."

2 Timothy 1 : 14.
" (14) As for the precious thing entrusted to you,

200

protect it with the help of the Holy Spirit who dwells within us."

1 John 4 : 12 - 13.
" (12) No one has ever seen God with human eyes; but if we love one

another, God truly lives in us. Consequently God's love has accomplished its mission among us. (13) How can we be sure that He truly lives in us and that we truly live

202

in Him? By one fact
: He has given us
His Spirit."

204

205

207

208

209

210

211

212

213

6.

A quick look at the very foundational premises of this book ' Holy Spirit of Love ?'

I thought it was very important to explain the foundational premises that this very book is based upon. The main premise , is that, the Holy Spirit is a gift of and from the Father and the Son of God, the Lord Jesus Christ. Therefore, He is not something which can be bought or sold or just acquired by anybody? This is important to see

and grasp from
the very outset of
the considerations
of this book about
the ' Holy Spirit
of Love.' In our
days and in our
generations
people have a
tendency to
believe otherwise

about the Holy Spirit?

The second major premise , is that, the gift of the Holy Spirit was poured out on all flesh because the Lord Jesus Christ went

220

to the Cross of Calvary. As is evidenced by the verses cited from the Gospel of John. Furthermore, the Holy Spirit was given to some people of God in the Old Testament

but with the Cross
of Jesus Christ
and His return to
the Father, the
Holy Spirit is now
poured out on all
flesh , as per Joel.

Thirdly, the
premise of this
book , is that, the

222

gift and gifting of the Holy Spirit is intimately tied up with the Love of God? All of which is why the book is called the ' Holy Spirit of Love.' In the end, the gift and gifting of the Holy Spirit will

223

and should by it's very nature make you fall more and more in Love with the Lord God Almighty and people in general. If the gift and gifting of the Holy Spirit does not do this, then you …

224

wonder if in reality you have the Holy Spirit, the Third person of the Trinity? The reason I say this, is because the Cross of Calvary and Jesus Christ going to it is all wrapped in the very LOVE OF THE LORD GOD ALMIGHTY. By the Lord Jesus Christ going through it's ugliness and cruelty we can receive the gift and the gifting of the Holy Spirit.

The last foundational premise of this very book, is that, in our days and in our very generations there is a crying need for people to ....

operate and out of the ' Holy Spirit of Love.' All too often the demonstrations of the gift and gifting of the Holy Spirit are done with a lot of power and at

times with little of
LOVE. In the end,
it is believed by
myself that the
very essence of
the Holy Spirit,
His operations,
gift and gifting , is
in fact LOVE.
Finally, in relation

to this, because His essence is LOVE, He will always point people who may well be far away from the Lord Jesus Christ to the Lord Jesus Christ. He will lift and magnify

the name and
renown of the
Lord Jesus Christ
at all times and in
all circumstances.
It is like He does
not want to bring
attention to
Himself but rather
to the Lord!

232

233

234

235

236

237

238

239

240

241

7.

Within this chapter we will spend time looking at the verses from the Gospel of John.

To begin with I want us to think about the very reality that the Holy Spirit was sent and poured out on all believer's because the Lord Jesus Christ did not want us to be orphans? In various versions in verse 18 of John 14 , the word the Lord Jesus Christ uses is translated as 'orphans '. Or as some have it He did not want us to be alone; without His presence in our lives? It would seem to me that it is all caught up with LOVE, both from the Father, the Son of God and even dare I say, the Holy Spirit Himself. The gift and gifting of the Holy Spirit demonstrates the very LOVE of the Godhead for those

who follow the Lord
Jesus Christ. Take
a moment and
think in your own
mind's eye what
your own life as a
follower of the Lord
Jesus Christ would
be like without the
very presence of
the Holy Spirit ? It

248

would like we were being orphaned and cut off from the very Presence of the Lord God Almighty, the Father , the Son of God and the Holy Spirit Himself.

I would see the verses from John 14 : 15 - 19 as very

249

much like
' promises from the
Lord Jesus Christ
about the very
coming and pouring
out of the Holy
Spirit upon all
those who would
follow Him.' Not
only does He does
not want us to be
as orphans ;

also He is making some very real and even earthy promises about the coming realities of the Holy Spirit in the lives of those who would follow Him.

There is a hint that the Holy Spirit

guarantees the return of the Lord Jesus Christ, the Second Coming and His abiding presence in the very lives of those who would follow Him. The gift and the gifting of the Holy Spirit is like

the down payment
on all of this
becoming a reality
and happening in
real time. As an
aside , we need to
understand that
the Third person of
the Trinity, the
Holy Spirit, is God.
Which is why we

253

can have the abiding presence of the Lord God Almighty, the Father, the Son of God and the Holy Spirit when we become follower's of the Lord Jesus Christ.

Finally in this chapter we need to consider that the Holy Spirit is actually the Spirit of Truth? This is all caught with John 15 : 26 and the coming of the ' Helper ' the Spirit of Truth. It is also caught with the

notion of this book
of the ' Holy Spirit
of Love ?' Because
He is the Spirit of
Truth, He also
reveals the very
reality of the fact
that the Lord God
Almighty loves us
as follower's of the
Lord Jesus Christ,

in that, he wants to lead us into the Truth about the Lord God Almighty? If He was not the 'Holy Spirit of Love'; He would not be wanting to lead into the Truth about the Lord God Almighty. Therefore;

being the Spirit of
Truth and the ' Holy
Spirit of Love ' go
together hand in
hand. Truth and
Love are to be found
in and through the
Holy Spirit of God.

Also, finally it is
worth noting that
the Holy Spirit is the

258

ONE who speaks and testifies to our spirit's about the Lord Jesus Christ. As can be seen in John 15 : 26. The 'Holy Spirit of Love' is all about speaking about the Lord Jesus Christ, His life , death and

His resurrection from the dead, on the third day. So, the Holy Spirit, will by His very nature always point a person to the works of the Lord Jesus Christ upon the Cross of Calvary and beyond it , to

260

His resurrection from the dead. In the end, the ' Holy Spirit of Love ' is all about putting the very spotlight on the Lord Jesus Christ and His works on our behalf. It's all about the Lord Jesus Christ !

262

263

264

265

266

267

268

269

8.

In this chapter we will spend some time in consideration of the verses from Romans 5 : 5 , 8 : 15 - 16 and 8 : 26 - 27 ?

270

The verses from Romans could in reality be the centerpiece verses of this particular book. They are all profound and telling in relation to this book. Romans 5 : 5 has to do with the love of God being in

our very hearts
through the vehicle
of the ' Holy Spirit
of Love?' It is very
reality that we have
the Holy Spirit in
our own hearts and
lives that testifies to
the very reality of
the Love of God for
us. Both the very

272

eality of the Love of God and the Holy Spirit Himself, are in fact gifts and gifting from the Lord God Almighty. Us becoming aware of the LOVE of GOD for us is a gift, in itself from the Lord God Almighty. It is the gift of the Holy Spirit;

that both makes this
LOVE real and also
seals it within us as
follower's of the
Lord Jesus Christ.

      If that were
not enough, let us
consider what
Romans 8 : 15 - 16
has to say to us ?

This takes the love idea so much further and develops it in a way we may not have been anticipating as readers of Romans? Not only do we have the LOVE of GOD but also through the Holy Spirit we are

now seen as being
' children of God?'
We can rightly now,
through the Holy
Spirit being in us cry
out 'Abba, Father';
to Father God. It is
like the Holy Spirit
and His presence in
our lives as
follower's of the ....

276

Lord Jesus Christ allows us to be recognized as children of God and as also having the right to call Him ' Abba or Father?' If you want , the Holy Spirit testifies with our spirit that we are in fact both

LOVED BY GOD
AND GOD'S
CHILDREN as well.
Both are in and of
themselves
amazing things
that the Holy Spirit
Himself, as God
does for us as
follower's of the
Lord Jesus Christ.

278

All of which is at the heart of why follow the Lord Jesus Christ and come to accept His work upon the Cross of Calvary for you and myself and for all humanity who accept Him.

Our journey in

Romans is not over ; we still need to consider the implications of Romans 8 : 26 - 27. These verses take a very different tack from the rest of what we have already dealt with in Romans. They are concerned primarily with the work of the Holy Spirit in helping us to pray as follower's of the Lord Jesus Christ in accordance with the very will of the Lord God. It is in our own weakness that the Holy Spirit, when He is present within us steps in and helps us to pray in accordance with the will of the Lord God Almighty. Apart from Him because of our own weakness we would not know how to pray to the Lord ...

282

God Almighty
according to his
desires, intentions
and revealed will.

I would also
believe that it is
because the Holy
Spirit loves us and
wants what is best
for us that He helps

283

us in our weakness
regarding prayer.
The love of the Lord
God Almighty is seen
in both the guidance
and empowerment
of the Holy Spirit
regarding how ,
when and what we
should be praying to
the Father , the Son

284

and the Holy Spirit, who Himself is God. Truly, the Holy Spirit is the ' Holy Spirit of Love ?' He lets us know we are loved by the Father and also how to pray to Him as we seek Him in prayer!

285

286

287

289

291

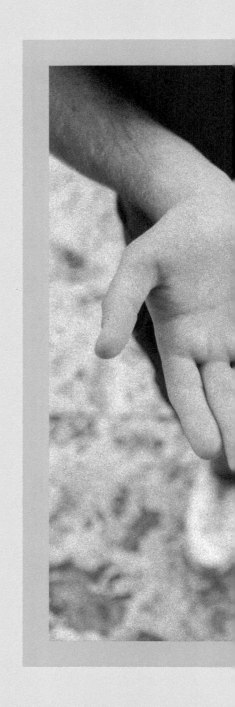

292

293

9.

In this chapter I want to consider the verses from 1 and 2 Corinthians and see what they have to say to us about the

294

Holy Spirit and the 'Holy Spirit of Love' in particular? Looking at notions such Wisdom and the temple of the Holy Spirit and what they have to do with the Spirit?

The first notion I want to deal with is the imagery of us as follower's of the Lord Jesus Christ being temples of the Holy Spirit. There is some variation in the translations of 1 Corinthians 3 : 16 -

17 and whether it is the Church corporately who is the temple of the Holy Spirit; or is it individual follower's of the Lord who are the Temple of the Holy Spirit? Whatever way you land , you

have here the image of the follower's or follower of the Lord Jesus Christ being the very temple of the Holy Spirit. No longer does the Lord God Almighty dwell in a man - made Temple but now He dwells in ..

298

the follower's of the Lord Jesus Christ; in their bodies, which are now temples of the Holy Spirit. You are in reality the very temple of the Holy Spirit, which is why one should keep their temple Holy and pure?

In the end, we are God's temple because we have the gift , as promised by the Lord Jesus Christ, of the Holy Spirit living and residing within us. Just think about it you are the very temple

300

of the ' Holy Spirit of Love ' ... It is within you and me that He resides upon this earth ! We get the gift of Him, the ' Holy Spirit of Love ' when we accept and come and abide each day with the

Lord Jesus Christ as both our LORD and SAVIOR!

There is also in the 1 Corinthians verses the notion of the Wisdom of the Lord God being contrasted with the very wisdom of the

World and it's rulers. It is in the end the Holy Spirit who does in reality reveal to us as follower's of the Lord Jesus Christ, the very Wisdom of God about and through the Lord Jesus Christ.

There is also a contrast made between the one who receives the spirit of the world and the one who receives the Holy Spirit. The one with the spirit of the world cannot receive the gifts ,

304

and gifting of the
Holy Spirit; it is
rather given to
those who follow,
abide and are in
relationship with
the Lord Jesus
Christ. The gifts
and gifting of the
Holy Spirit are seen
as being nonsense
by the one who has

the spirit of the world rather than the Holy Spirit.

It is worth noting at this point that the gifts and gifting that are not understood by those with the spirit of the world are rooted in

both the LOVE OF
GOD and the ' Holy
Spirit of Love ?'
The very gifts and
gifting and even
the very Wisdom of
the Lord God
Almighty are all
caught up with and
enmeshed in the
very love of the
Holy Spirit!

307

Finally in this chapter we need to consider the import of 2 Corinthians 5 : 5 (GNT) " (5) God is the one who has prepared us for this change, and he gave us his Spirit as the guarantee of all ...

that has in store for us. " The change the verse talks about is into our heavenly bodies , as per the verses beforehand? Again, we have this notion of the ' Holy Spirit of Love ' acting as a guarantee of the future, our future in the Lord God Almighty and in his Heaven.

Not only that but the ' Holy Spirit of Love ' also guarantee's that what the Word of

310

God promises regarding Heaven and the Heavenly City, the New Jerusalem and our part in it all , will in fact happen. It's like through the Holy Spirit the Lord God Almighty has guaranteed it all !

311

312

313

314

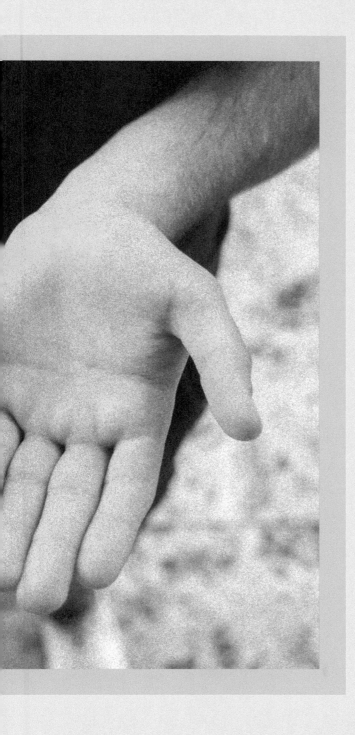

315

316

317

318

319

10.

Let us now consider
Galatians 5 : 16 - 18
and what it has to
say to us about the
' Holy Spirit of
Love ?'

320

This verse talks about the ways that the Holy Spirit and the Human Nature within us are at war. These verses occur in a section of verses dealing with the Law and ends in verse 18 with the reality that we are not subject to the Law.

In many ways, these verses deal with the battle that takes place between the flesh, the human nature and the Holy Spirit. They make the point that they are diametrically opposed to each other. All of which is another reason why we need the Holy Spirit, the 'Holy Spirit of Love'. He will lead us to do things that are not what the human nature wants . In themselves some things are wrong and sinful according to the Law of the Lord God Almighty, the Human Nature left to it's own devices.

In these verses we are given a very real contrast between a person led by the Human Nature and one led by the Holy Spirit. With the injunction that those who have the Holy Spirit are not subject to the law, the section of verses ends. The emphasis is on the person being led by the Holy Spirit and not just..

325

being led by their human nature. The implication seems to be that one can have the Holy Spirit and not be led by the Holy Spirit. If this is the case , then, one is being led purely by their own Human Nature?

The implication is that, if one has only the human nature they cannot do what the Lord God Almighty wants or commands in His Law. If one is not led by the Holy Spirit this is true as well for the person.

328

331

332

333

334

335

11.

Let us now consider Galatians 5 : 22 - 2? and the notion of the fruit of the Holy Spirit, the ' Holy Spirit of Love '?

Galatians 5 : 22 - 23 (GNT) "(22) But the Spirit produces love, joy, peace, patience, kindness, goodness, faithfulness,

(23) humility, and self - control. There is no law against such things as these. "

It is the ' Holy Spirit', the ' Holy Spirit of Love ' that does in fact produce the fruit of the Spirit within us. It's worth noting that the Holy Spirit, the ' Holy Spirit of Love' also produces love within us as well. All

338

the positive fruit of the Holy Spirit come from having the Holy Spirit within us. We in and of ourselves cannot even hope to produce the fruit of the Holy Spirit without the Holy Spirit. It's like ....

in some ways, asking an apple tree to produce apples by just thinking about producing apples .... In the end, it does not happen like that and the reality of it , is that, we need the Holy Spirit to ...

340

produce the fruit of the Holy Spirit within us as follower's of the Lord Jesus Christ.

In some ways, ' There is no law against such things as these'; sums up the very reality of the fruit of the Holy

Spirit being counter intuitive to the Law and it's keeping and any attempt to be saved through the very keeping of it. In the end, there is no Law against the fruit of the Holy Spirit and the very fruit He produces in the life of a follower of the Lord Jesus Christ.

Finally, as someone once said there is no Law against LOVE! All of which is why we need the 'Holy Spirit of Love' to produce more love and fruit in us!

344

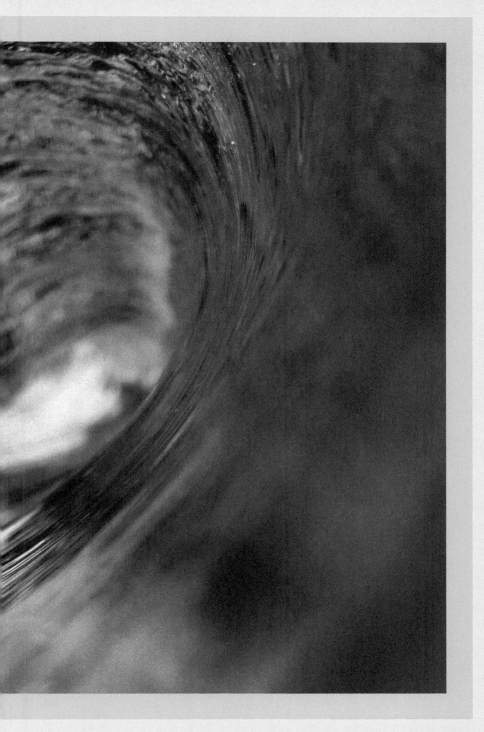

345

346

347

348

349

350

351

352

353

12.

I want to finish with the verses from 1 John 4 : 12 - 13. These verses focus on LOVE as well !

354

It would seem that these verses from 1 John 4 : 12 - 13 are a fantastic way to wind up and conclude this book; the ' Holy Spirit of Love'. In these verses we are presented with the notion that if we ..

love one another , then we can see the Lord God Almighty in the very act of the LOVE that we have for one another. It is based on the premise that the very essence of the Lord God Almighty is actually

LOVE!

Here is the verses from 1 John 4 : 12 - 13 (GNT)

" (12) No one has ever seen God, but if we love one another, God lives in union with us, and his love is .....

made perfect in us.
(13) We are sure
that we live in
union with God and
that he lives in
union with us,
because he has
given us his
Spirit. " As we can
see from the verses
the very real test ..

358

of both our union
with the Lord God
Almighty and
having the Holy
Spirit is LOVE for
one another. In
some ways, it is a
very circular
argument, if one
loves others who
are follower's of

the Lord Jesus Christ , then, one is in union with the Lord God Almighty and also has the Holy Spirit dwelling inside of them.

Just like the fruit of the Holy Spirit, we cannot in

anyway, shape or form just think we have the Holy Spirit living and dwelling inside of us . It is rather when there is evidence shown by us in loving others of the Body of Christ that proves that we have both a viable union with the Lord God Almighty by the Holy Spirit Himself and the very presence of the Holy Spirit dwelling inside of us.

There is a surety in both , by

having and even
receiving the gift
and gifting of the
Holy Spirit. This
occurs, or should
occur when we
receive the Lord
Jesus Christ as our
own Lord and
Savior. Yet, as in the
Book of Acts , it can

happen after this event in our own lives ... I would believe that everybody receives the Holy Spirit when they are saved . Yet, it is also possible for people and individual's to receive Him in His fullness , in terms of the gift of Him and His gifting at a later stage? In all of this , let us not dictate to the Lord God Almighty and the person of the Trinity, the Holy Spirit. In the end, I am not sure one ...

size or event or way
of doing things
works with the
giving and the
coming of the very
Holy Spirit upon
people who get
saved by the Lord
Jesus Christ.

It may well be

the fullness of the
Holy Spirit comes
into a particular
individual's life at a
later stage after they
have been saved by
the Lord Jesus
Christ? In the end, it
really the ' Holy
Spirit of Love 'that is
given to the person!

As we have seen from these verses from 1 John 4 : 12 - 13; it is love for each other that both reveals the Lord God Almighty to us and also whether in reality we have the Holy Spirit indwelling us?

368

All of which is why write a book with the title the ' Holy Spirit of Love.' The very love we have for each other as followers of the Lord Jesus Christ reveals both our own union with the Lord God Almighty and the

very presence of the
indwelling of the
Holy Spirit within
us.

Finally, in the
end , we also need to
remember that the
Holy Spirit Himself
is a very real gift
from the Lord God

Almighty. He is not and will never be someone or a spirit, the 'Holy Spirit of Love ' , that we can attain by ourselves or even by our own good works and effort before the very gaze of the Lord God Almighty!

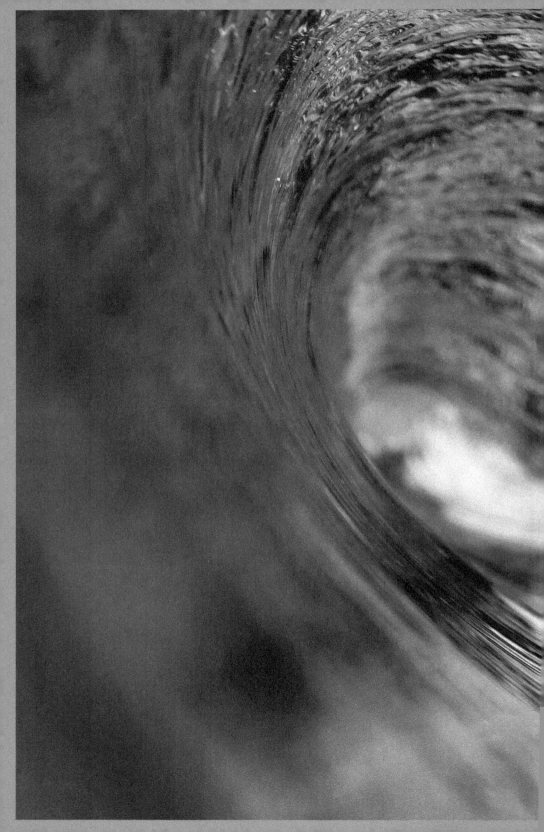

376

377

378

379

380

381

382

383

Epilogue :

There has been an attempt made throughout this very book to talk and discuss the 'Holy Spirit of Love.' Looking at and thinking about this in terms of various verses from the Word of God.

In the end, we saw how the gift of and the gifting of the Holy Spirit is something that is rooted in the very LOVE of the Godhead itself. The very essence of the Lord God Almighty is LOVE and the very essence of the Third Person, the Holy Spirit is LOVE as well!

A prayer you might want to pray to the Lord God Almighty, at this very moment in time is :

Dear Lord Jesus Christ ... Thank you for giving us the gift and gifting of the Holy Spirit! May I walk in ..

386

the Holy Spirit and the very love of the Lord God Almighty that is at the heart of His very essence, in my own life before the gaze of the Father, the Lord God Almighty !

AMEN !!!!

The
Author :

John C Burt

388

389

JOHN IS BETWEEN CHURCHES AT THE MOMENT. HE STILL ATTENDS CHURCH ON A SUNDAY!

390

John loves coffee,
pizza and chicken
and jellyfish, in that
order ! The coffee
has to be strong,
hot and frothy in
it's nature !

391

AMEN!

and

AMEN!!!

SHALOM :

MAY THE VERY REAL PEACE OF THE LORD JESUS CHRIST BE WITH US ALL!

AMEN...

393

394

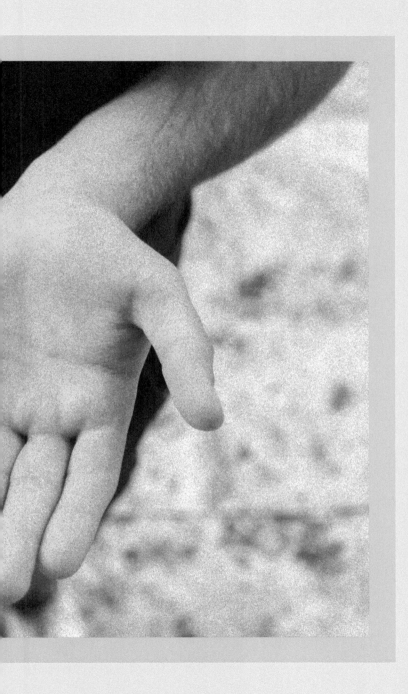

395

396

397